PRAYER THAT WORKS

A Step-by-Step Guide to
Writing Your Prayers
and Seeing Answers

LAURA DOMINO

Prayer That Works

Copyright © 2021 Laura Domino

All rights reserved. No part of this publication may be reproduced, stored in a retrieval system, or transmitted in any form or by any means—electronic, mechanical, photocopy, recording or any other—except for brief quotations in printed reviews, without the prior permission of the author.

The content in this book is intended to be inspirational and does not promise a guaranteed outcome. Results will vary. The reader assumes all responsibility for the use of the information in this text. The author shall not be liable for any negative experience anyone has regarding reading this book.

Scriptures taken from the Holy Bible, New International Version®, NIV®. Copyright ©1973, 1978, 1984, 2011 by Biblica, Inc.™ Used by permission of Zondervan. All rights reserved worldwide. www.zondervan.com The "NIV" and "New International Version" are trademarks registered in the United States Patent and Trademark Office by Biblica, Inc.™

TABLE OF CONTENTS

INTRODUCTION	1
CHAPTER ONE: Start with your need.	5
CHAPTER TWO: Discover how has God provided for others.	13
CHAPTER THREE: Remember who you are to God.	19
CHAPTER FOUR: Consider what God has already done for you.	23
CHAPTER FIVE: Write what you're asking for.	27
CHAPTER SIX: Write God's response.	30
CHAPTER SEVEN: Become accountable.	35
CHAPTER EIGHT: Wait for the answer.	38
CONCLUSION: Write about your love for God.	41
SUMMARY	42
ABOUT THE AUTHOR	47

INTRODUCTION

If I told you that you would double your income by using this book, you would probably follow all of my instructions to find out how much money you can earn. However, I'm not going to make that claim. That's not what this book is for.

This book was written to help you get excited about meeting with God daily. As I began writing this, I wanted to motivate, inspire, and encourage you to lean into God. Get "whisper-close" to the God who loves you more than anyone else.

That's the beauty of prayer, and that's what the twelve tips in this book are meant to help with. If you take this book seriously and act on the twelve tips in this step-by-step process, you will make positive changes in your prayer life. When you see growth in your prayer life, you'll see that growth reflected in other areas of your life as well.

Use each tip, one by one, at your own pace, so you can look back after a month of progress and see specific areas in your life that have begun to transform.

To see your success, you will need:

- this book
- a prayer journal
- a Bible
- and a pen or pencil

The purpose of a prayer journal is to write your prayers so you can read them later and see how God has moved in your life.

If you need a prayer journal, I've created one that works especially well with this book. It's called **The Prayer That Works Journal: 31 Days Of Writing Your Prayers.** It's easy to use and contains space to write your notes as you go through the chapters.

In your prayer journal, write both your requests and God's answers to prayer. Recording conversations between you and God will take a little time and patience if you're not used to it. If this is new to you, just follow the steps in this book and see how God guides you in your relationship with Him.

As you start this book, make sure you have a relationship with God. If you feel like God has never answered your prayers, your first step is to look at your life and find a connection to God in all of the major intersections or turning points.

If you still can't find how God has shown you direction in the past, don't worry. Your eyes can be opened to the instruction God has already been pouring into your life. If you haven't seen it yet, that doesn't mean you won't ever see it.

If you don't have a relationship with God, it's easy to begin one right now.

Read about the criminal on the cross.

In Luke 23:32-43, we read about two criminals who were crucified next to Jesus. The first one hurled insults at Jesus, but the second admitted his guilt and said that Jesus had done nothing wrong. The second criminal asked Jesus to remember him. Jesus responded, "Truly I tell you, today you will be with me in paradise."

The second criminal probably wasn't a member of a church. He probably hadn't spent countless hours volunteering and donating to charities. He had just admitted that he was receiving the judgment he deserved because he had committed a crime.

But Jesus accepted the second criminal.

Jesus didn't wait for him to start doing good works. Ephesians 2:8-9 explains, "For it is by grace you have been saved, through faith—and this is not from yourselves, it is the gift of God—not by works, so that no one can boast."

Although Jesus was being crucified with two sinners, they weren't the only sinners he died for. He died for all of us. Romans 5:8 tells us, "But God demonstrates his own love for us in this: While we were still sinners, Christ died for us."

God already accepts us.

When Jesus asks people to follow him, he doesn't look for perfect people. He seeks out people who have willing and honest hearts, people who are open to being changed by a relationship with Him.

All God asks of us is a response to his invitation.

Invitation #1: Will you let me take away your sins?

Why would anyone avoid having the stain of sin removed? Unfortunately, we all have moments of vigorously holding onto our sins. Out of shame, some of us hold our sins behind our backs, not wanting to admit that we did such a thing. Out of distrust, some of us won't let Jesus have our sin because we're afraid that the sin will have our name on it forever.

Our reluctance to admit our sins or even our blindness to our sins leads to arrogance, which is another sin. We look at our past and see that we haven't been criminals like the men on the cross beside Jesus, so we don't want to wear the label of "sinner." But we have sinned. All of us have sinned.

God can wash away the stain of sin, guilt, and shame. Jesus has already dealt with the sin of mankind. Once and for all, he has paid the price for us to be free of all of it. But God demands a response from us. Our salvation is ready for us to receive, but it requires our acceptance of what Jesus did for us.

Our eternal freedom is determined by us. We have to accept Jesus.

Jesus hung on the cross for our sins, not his. He didn't have any sins. His sacrifice for our salvation was a gift to us.

We must accept the gift.

Invitation #2: Will you walk with me?

Once you have accepted God's gift and the saving of your soul, you begin to learn more about living in the love of God. You are beginning a new relationship, one that must be attended to in order to be maintained properly.

Spiritual growth happens when you study who God is and what He has said. That takes Bible study and prayer.

If you walk with Him in your daily life, your relationship thrives. That is what this book is for. Its purpose is to help you improve your relationship with God so you can become more mature in spiritual understanding and better enjoy the abilities and gifts God gives you.

When you are flourishing in your relationship with God, you learn much more than you thought possible.

Amazing things happen when you put a lot of effort into your relationship with God.

CHAPTER ONE

Start with your need.

Learning about prayer is a process. It will be a different journey for each of us. We can make the most of our efforts by going through the twelve tips in this book with a determination to connect with God and grow spiritually in this process.

Not everyone prays daily. If you do, you're well on your way to some exciting spiritual growth. If you don't pray daily, you can still join me in this learning adventure.

Most people go back to praying after a long time away from prayer simply because there is something they need that they can't get on their own. A lot of people pray for more money. God obviously doesn't give out money every time someone asks. He's our Heavenly Father, not a vending machine.

If you're a parent and your children only came to talk to you when they needed something, how would that make you feel?

I'm a parent. I remember the giggles and snuggles with my little ones. They didn't worry about what they needed because they knew their parents would provide for them all of their meals and clothing and entertainment. They came to us to tell us something that was important to them.

One day, my child couldn't wait to tell me what happened. "Today at school, I sat in a police car!" I already knew something like that might happen because I had received communications from the school that it was Community Helper Week. That day, a local officer came by the school to give the kids a close-up view of a real police car. However, it was so much more fun to hear from my child about how her day went.

God is ready to listen to you.

When we pray to God, we don't always have a major struggle to pray about. We might just be letting God know how we feel about something. We might need to express our opinions or share the joy about what happened that day. When you have a relationship with God, don't ever complain of loneliness because He's always there.

What do you need?

Some people need money. There are all kinds of fund-raising opportunities for people these days. I've seen social media posts with links to GoFundMe or Kickstarter or similar websites. But if you're pressed for time, coming up short, and can't pay a bill, you might feel like asking God for a financial miracle.

Some people need healing. There are so many examples of how Jesus healed people in the Bible. There is no formula that explains how to get God to heal you. He made your body, and he can fix it. The human body isn't going to last forever. We go through stages of aging. This world has disease in it. People make mistakes and have accidents. We pray for ourselves, and we pray for others to receive healing. Sometimes healing miracles take time.

Most people need God's wisdom for making decisions. When God doesn't hear from some people, it might be because they think they're able to control their circumstances. Then when they experience an opportunity or a challenging situation that requires a difficult decision, they run to God for help. The prayer is usually about how they can't see a solution to their problem. What was controllable has started to feel out of control.

We all need a stronger relationship with God. If we're not looking for extra money, a supernatural healing, or a miracle answer that will solve all our problems, maybe we're hungering for something that we can't express. Maybe we're not satisfied with life because we have what we need, but we're still not happy. If we're trying to fill our lives with things that others seem to be happy with but we still feel empty, maybe we should look at how much attention we're giving to our relationships with God.

Why are you asking for things?

Some of our prayers are about meeting needs that we understand, but sometimes we don't know what to pray for. We just know we need help from Almighty God, the Creator who already knows everything.

If we're praying about something we don't understand, we may need to change how we see the problem.

If we step back from the problems we can't solve, we can see them differently. We often need a change of perspective before we pray.

Writing in a journal will help us see more clearly what we're asking for. We can narrow down to specifics later, but for now let's look at the big picture.

What affects our prayers?

Emotions affect our prayers. If you don't agree, think about how emotions affect our conversations with family and friends. Two high school girls who found out they both made it onto the list of varsity cheerleaders will hug, jump, and screech their conversation with each other. In 2 Samuel 6:14, David rejoiced, dancing before the Lord with all his might. His physical act of celebration was communication to God because sometimes words aren't enough.

But most people don't pray to God when they're rejoicing.

Think back to major tragedies like the collapse of the World Trade Center towers. The news media covered the story from many angles and reported that 2,763 lives were lost. American pain was so bad that people stood in line to enter churches. Natural disasters like the heat wave of 1988 cost $120 billion in damages and thousands of deaths. Hurricane Harvey produced $125 billion in damages and 107 deaths. Hurricane Katrina produced $125 billion in damages and 1,836 deaths. These events drove people to their knees in prayer. We pulled together in groups and asked God for help.

We pray because something is not right.

Pain affects our prayers. We're either experiencing pain or helping a loved one through their pain. I remember being severely dehydrated and in pain. It was hard to communicate with the nurse who stood near me with a confused expression on her face. I tried to say, "My eye hurts." I don't know what she heard, but my message was being affected by my body's response to pain.

Pain is your body's communication that something isn't right. When we get that signal from our bodies, we immediately go through a checklist of things that could be wrong. Just like a mother questioning her crying child, we question our bodies. Is there a bruise or a scrape? Did I eat the wrong thing? Once we figure out the source of the pain, we are better able to deal with the problem.

As a mother, I sometimes found it hard to figure out why my children were crying. If the children were old enough to talk, I tried to get them to stop crying and tell me why they were upset. I could help them quicker if I knew what had happened. When my children discussed with me why they were having pain, I could help them avoid it and prevent pain in the future. For example, if a child tripped over a toy, the solution isn't to step over toys more carefully. A better solution is to pick up the toys and put them in a place where no one will trip over them.

Prayer is like that. If we're praying for God to relieve us of pain, we might be asking for the wrong thing.

Jealousy affects our prayers. If you have the temptation to be jealous of people who seem to pray and get what they want right away, watch out. That's a detour you don't want to make.

That jealousy is based on the lie that God loves them more than he loves you. Listening to lies will postpone your blessings.

God loves you whether you need money or healing or nothing at all. He doesn't give some people money because he loves them more. He can't love one person more than another because he loves each of us as much as possible. He loves them the same as he loves you—with everything he's got.

Don't hide your jealousy when you're writing in your journal. Talk to God in your journal about the things you want to change.

Jealousy is something that can change. It's from the evil forces that want to hide your blessings in their darkness. The best way to disperse the darkness is to shine light on it.

Writing in your journal about experiencing jealousy will help you put some light on the situation. The light of God will make the darkness flee.

> *Dear God,*
>
> *I feel jealous when I see (this person) getting her prayers answered ahead of mine. I know it's wrong not to like her because of her answered prayers. My desire is to fix my relationship with her before jealousy ruins it. Therefore, I confess to You these jealous feelings and ask for Your forgiveness. And I ask You to continue to protect (this person) so that she doesn't lose any of her blessings. I choose to support her with my friendship while I wait for my prayers to be answered. I can do that, God, because Your love is in me. I can do all things through Your power in me because You give me strength. I thank You for working in me to bring to completion all the blessings You've planted in me.*

Tip #1: List your needs.

List the things you are praying for. Go ahead and make that list right now in your prayer journal.

What are your priorities?

Looking at your list will help you get a better view of the priorities in your prayers. If your priorities are off, fix those first.

One way to look at the priorities on your prayer list is to make a note of the root of the problem.

Many times, we don't know the root of the problem.

Take a look at the list you've just made. Divide the list between things you want (like a winning lottery ticket) and problems you want solved (like healing from sickness).

When you review the items on the list of things you want, look for the items that you can delete from your list. For example, asking for money or a winning lottery ticket won't solve any problems. If debt is the problem and you win the lottery, your problem won't be automatically solved. You could spend the lottery money on having fun and still be in debt. It's like cutting off the leaves of a tree that you want removed. Stop cutting off the leaves of the tree and start uprooting the problem.

Changing bad habits, losing weight, and getting out of debt are all things that can be done successfully, but it takes work.

God knows our weaknesses. He knows why we have some of our prayer requests. He knows our needs better than we do. He might be waiting for us to understand what we should be praying for.

God may withhold things you're praying for to save you from yourself. If God took away your pain every time you asked, you might not ever solve the problem that's causing the pain.

Don't just ask for pain relief if you have a broken arm. Ask the doctor to fix the broken arm.

Tip #2: Make corrections with God's help.

Look at the list of your prayer requests and ask God to help you see the list as He sees it. Ask for His guidance and make corrections to your list as you receive understanding. God's priorities are not the same as ours. He can help us focus on the important items.

Be patient. Ask for wisdom and understanding before you cry out to God about His unwillingness to give you what you want.

God is willing.

"Ask and it will be given to you..." Read Matthew 7:7-12 to see how eager God is to review your prayer list with you.

After we ask God for wisdom and help with priorities, then we can ask God to put His desires in our hearts. Humbling ourselves to ask what He wants us to have will help us get what we really need.

In the next chapter, let's take a look at how God has answered the prayers of others.

Chapter 1 Action List

1. Make the most of your efforts by going through the twelve tips in this book with a determination to connect with God and grow spiritually in this process.
2. Create a list of the things you are praying for.
3. Discover the priorities in your prayers.
4. Ask God for wisdom and understanding to correct your prayer list.
5. Ask God to help us see what is His will for us.

CHAPTER TWO

Discover how has God provided for others.

In order to find what God has done to provide for others with your need, look in the Bible. If you don't have a concordance in your personal library, you can use your computer to do a search for keywords at BibleGateway.com

If you need healing, type words in the search bar and keep changing your keywords in the search bar until you find the verses that apply to the healing you're praying for. Rather than typing "healing," type "heal" to give you more Scriptures to browse through in your search.

Tip #3 Find cases of answered prayer.

Do you know how God has already answered prayers for healing?

There are examples of God healing people throughout the Bible. There are more examples in medical journals and newspaper articles. Have you seen blogs written by people who have been miraculously healed by God? Since healing miracles are so numerous, let's focus on the Old Testament examples.

How did God heal people in the Old Testament?

Naaman's story of healing is found in 2 Kings 5:1-14. Naaman, a highly respected soldier and commander of the army, was sent to the prophet Elisha's house to receive healing. However, Elisha didn't come out of his house and greet Naaman. Elisha sent a messenger to deliver instructions, which was vastly different from the reception that Naaman was used to. In order to get his healing, Naaman had to humble himself and obey the instructions of the prophet without seeing him face-to-face.

Which books of the Bible have stories of people receiving miracles? Notice that there is a pattern of humility before God. In the first chapter of Nehemiah, his prayer begins with confession of sin, not just his, but also the sins of his father's family and other Israelites. He brought his honesty and humility to God before he brought a request to God.

Proverbs 15 gives insight for those who want their prayers answered. Verses 8, 9, and 29 mention those who know God is listening to their prayers. Verse 33 tells how to have the right attitude in prayer. We are to fear the Lord and show respect because "humility comes before honor." Having an attitude of humility in your prayers shows that you've received wisdom from God.

Hosea 14 shows a picture of God's mercy and desire to restore His people, but it begins with repentance.

But what about the healing miracles of Jesus?

In Matthew 8, we read the story of the centurion who asked Jesus to heal his servant. He asked and believed it would be done. "But just say the word, and my servant will be healed." Jesus was delighted that the centurion showed such great faith in front of Jesus' disciples, who weren't always known for having great faith.

It's important to know what God has already done before you ask God how He will answer your prayer. Knowing how far God will go to bring someone the healing their body needs builds your confidence that God will go to great lengths to bring you healing too.

Start writing your story.

Don't just pick a random story in the Bible and follow the instructions given to that person. God is developing your faith to tell your own story.

Prayer That Works

Hebrews 11:6 tells us that "without faith it is impossible to please God, because anyone who comes to him must believe that he exists and that he rewards those who earnestly seek him." God waits for us to believe that He exists and that He loves us. When we cling to God as our Heavenly Father and not just a vending machine for our healing, it's easier for us to believe that healing from God is related to His unsurpassing love for us.

In the New Testament, the accounts of blind people being healed show that Jesus didn't do the same thing for every person. Jesus only acted and spoke as our Heavenly Father wanted.

> "Very truly I tell you, the Son can do nothing by himself; he can do only what he sees his Father doing, because whatever the Father does the Son also does." John 5:19

> "For I did not speak on my own, but the Father who sent me commanded me to say all that I have spoken. I know that his command leads to eternal life. So whatever I say is just what the Father has told me to say." John 12:49-50

There is an order of importance. First, find out what God wants. Second, do that.

If you need money to pay your taxes, look in the Bible for the verses that show how Jesus told his disciples to pull a coin from a fish's mouth to pay their taxes. Just to be clear, it wasn't the right fishing spot or the right fishing pole that helped them pay their taxes. It wasn't the fish at all. It was their obedience to God that helped them get what they needed.

If you need money to pay debt, look for the verses that show how the prophet told a woman to fill big pots full of oil and then sell them so she could have money to pay her debt. That verse will help you see the compassion of God for His people. That verse will help build your faith in the God who meets needs.

Do you need wisdom? Look for verses that speak to your need.

Now that you have a list of things you want and a list of problems you want to be free from, look for examples in the Bible of the things on your list.

Make a note beside your list with a Bible verse that shows how God has already provided for someone with similar needs.

Your prayer list might not include verses where people are asking for the exact items you're asking for, but take a moment and think it through. People are the same throughout time. We all need the same basic things. All parents want healing for their children and food for the table.

As you look for examples of how God has answered someone else's prayer or met their needs, you won't be asking God to meet your needs in the same way. Your list will remind you of how God has helped someone else. Select Scriptures that will help you focus on the fact that God knows your needs and knows how to meet them.

What do you expect from God?

If you have a list of things you're praying for and a few Bible verses written beside each one, you have a good starting point. You are ready to raise your expectation level.

Having a good relationship with God is essential when we're trying to believe that He wants to heal us. We can't let a bad doctor's report make us give up hope for our own healing. We can't let living in a poor neighborhood make us lose our determination to get out of debt.

We have to build our faith, not our doubt. Instead of letting our attention dwell on the people around us who are living with less than God's best, we can lift up our eyes to God and give our attention to His word. We can let God build our faith in what He can do.

If we are going to believe what God wants for us, we have to look at God.

Tip #4: Raise your expectation of God.

Your mind has to agree with God's desire to bless you. It may be easier to change your mindset if you picture yourself as a child in front of your Heavenly Father.

My children know I love them because we have a good relationship. I believe God gave me the experience of raising children so I could know what a parent's love feels like. I'm an imperfect parent, but I love my kids with all my heart. God is perfect. His love for me is much bigger than my love for my children could ever be.

If I want the very best for my kids, I know that God has even better things in mind for me—and all his children.

I can set my expectation pretty high after I read the Bible verses that show how God's love washed away my sin while I was still a rebellious sinner (Romans 5:8).

In the next chapter, let's take a look at who we are before we start asking God to give us what we want.

Chapter 2 Action List

1. Make a note by the list of the things you are praying for. Include Bible verses where people are asking for things similar to those on your prayer list.
2. Discover how God has answered prayers in the past.
3. Ask God to help you build your expectation to receive what He wants you to have.

CHAPTER THREE

Remember who you are to God.

Who do you think you are?

Many times, our prayers suffer from a case of mistaken identity. We don't know who we are.

Take a moment to make a list of all the things you are. This can be a list of items that describe you from God's perspective.

Tip #5: Look at how God sees you.

It's important to look at yourself from God's viewpoint to remember how He sees you before you pray.

He's not looking at you to see if your hair looks good. Physical appearance isn't going to persuade God to give or not give the things on your prayer list.

Think about how God sees you when you come to your prayer time. If you remember His perspective, you can see how beautiful you are to God before you pray.

If you do this, it will change how you pray.

Which things in your list tell *who* you are and which tell *what* you've done?

Are you a church member? Did you get a perfect attendance medal from your Sunday School class? This means nothing in the big picture. When Jesus spoke to the criminal on the cross next to him, He didn't ask him those questions.

Instead of temporary accolades, dig deeper into the things you've discovered about yourself since you accepted Jesus.

Separate the list items that point to you as an individual from those that point to you as having done something.

Write who you are, not what you've done. The prayer comes from a person, not from the accomplishments, not from the sins, and not from the bucket list.

> *"Yet to all who did receive him, to those who believed in his name, he gave the right to become children of God—" John 1:12*

> *"This is what the Lord says—your Redeemer, the Holy One of Israel: 'I am the Lord your God, who teaches you what is best for you, who directs you in the way you should go." Isaiah 48:17*

> *"On the day when I act," says the Lord Almighty, "they will be my treasured possession. I will spare them, just as a father has compassion and spares his son who serves him." Malachi 3:17*

Think about the things that make you who you are. My decisions reflect the kind of person I am. My decisions are based on my relationship with God. John 1:12 reminds me that I am important to God. I am a child of God. That's who I am.

And as a child of God, I listen for His loving correction. Isaiah 48:17 reminds me that learning from God has shaped me. I'm a student of God's ways. That's who I am.

When I notice God in my life, I feel cherished and valuable. Malachi 3:17 reminds me that God will watch over me because of who I am to Him.

Now look at your list and make a note of what each thing means to you. I'll start you off with three items that might be on your list.

I am a child of God: I enjoy the connection of belonging to God.

I am a student of God's ways: Pursuing God and being in His presence brings me joy.

I am a treasure: I feel cherished and loved by God.

In the next chapter, let's take a look at the ways God has already provided for you.

Chapter 3 Action List

1. Make a list of the things you are to God.
2. Make a note of what that means to you.

CHAPTER FOUR

Consider what God has already done for you.

Now that you know how God sees you, you have a glimpse of who He is. But we don't always see Him as we should.

> *"Whoever does not love does not know God, because God is love." 1 John 4:8*

Love is the very best word to describe God because God is love. Do we approach God with the understanding that He is love?

We approach God based on how we see Him.

Tip #6: Look at how you see God.

Let's discover how we really see God.

We can do that by looking at what we expected from God in Chapter Two.

Most of the time, our expectations come from what we've experienced. When we ask ourselves what God has already done for us, we have to dig into our memory for the ways God has blessed us so far.

Sadly, we tend to forget many of the things God has done for us. We receive blessings and move on to other things, much like a toddler unwrapping Christmas gifts.

Take a moment and make a list of things God has done in your life. When you complete that list, look at it and see if what you wrote makes God seem bigger or smaller.

In order to raise our expectations of God, we have to realize the truth of who we're praying to.

Who are you praying to?

Now make a list of things that describe how you see God. Separate the items that describe God as a person and those that describe His actions. The prayer goes to a person, not to the things He's done, not to the people God has created, not to the things you want, and certainly not to a vending machine.

After you have a good list of descriptions of who God is to you, make a note after each one that tells why you see God that way.

Here are some examples from my list:

In Genesis 22:14, I learned that God is my provider. I've never been hungry.

In Exodus 15:26, I learned that God is my healer. I've been healed by God, and He has worked through me to heal others.

In Joshua 1:9, I learned that God is my confidence and courage. I've been used by God to speak to many audiences.

In Leviticus 22:32, I learned that God is my holiness. God has protected me and kept me set apart, something I cannot do on my own.

In Isaiah 40:31, I learned that God is my strength. My husband and I have raised two children.

Now you know who you are to God and who God is to you. You can think about that relationship whenever you pray.

Having this close, responsive relationship with God will remind you of His powerful love and how much He wants to bless you.

This will also help you determine what to say in your prayers because when you get to know God, you become more aware of what kind of prayers you should be praying. If you know God better now, your prayers are better now.

Our prayers are informed by our relationship with Him.

In the next chapter, let's take a look at the specific things on your prayer list.

Chapter 4 Action List

1. List what God has done in your life.
2. List items that describe who God is to you.
3. Make a note of why you see God that way.

CHAPTER FIVE

Write what you're asking for.

What are you praying for? Separate your prayers for individuals and prayers for things. Most of the time, your prayers will be for a person (you), not for the things you want.

That may seem confusing to some, but look at it this way: God is more interested in building up your character so you can be strong and wise enough to make good decisions.

Tip # 7: Ask God how you should change.

Ask God how you need to change in order to be able to receive what He has for you. Do you need an attitude shift? Will a change in perspective help you pray for the right things? Can being open to coming changes help you be available to God's gifts? Do you need to make a change in your schedule to make room for taking new action?

These changes may put you in the right place at the right time. Not making changes may delay the miracle you've been longing for.

Remember that God looks on the heart and deals with each of us as we need to be directed.

Giving you money won't improve your spiritual understanding. Giving you a new car won't accomplish that.

Don't expect God to just give you stuff. He's more interested in you than in your financial success. He's looking at the condition of your heart before He acknowledges the condition of your bank account.

Make a list of the specific things you need. Don't generalize. Don't list categories of things. Create a list of clearly stated needs.

How are you asking?

The prayer goes to a person who loves you and knows what you need better than you do.

Why are you worried about getting the items on your list? What will happen if you don't get what you pray for?

Tip #8: Ask God to help you prioritize.

Will the things on your list make your life more comfortable? Is personal comfort the reason you're praying for them?

Before you list your items in order of importance, ask God for wisdom.

The things that are mainly on your list because it would make life easier are less important than the things that have an eternal impact.

Sometimes we get our hearts set on a temporary earthly pleasure. If it doesn't lead someone to Jesus, it's less important.

I'm not saying God doesn't want us to enjoy life while we're on this planet. We just have to allow God to remind us of His priorities.

Chapter 5 Action List

1. Ask God how you need to change in order to be able to receive what He wants to give you.

2. List what you're asking for. Be specific.

3. Consider what will happen if you don't get what you pray for.

4. Prioritize what you're asking for.

CHAPTER SIX

Write God's response.

So far, we've listed our problems and asked God to help us make corrections to our list. We've looked for examples of how God has answered prayers in the past and raised our expectation of what God may do.

Not only did we look at how God sees us, but we also looked at how we see God. We've asked God how we need to change and asked Him to help us prioritize what we're praying for.

What have we been missing?

Tip # 9: Listen to God's response.

Have you been listening to what God has been saying to you in response to your prayers?

We often pray as if we're ordering at a fast food restaurant. We throw our prayer lists to God in a rush and expect him to deliver in a hurry.

Our relationships with God would be better if we would take the time to sit with him and just be together. If we would slowly find out about each other through calm, loving conversation, the relationship would improve significantly.

The Lord confides in us.

When we stay humble before God and listen as we pray, we will hear the wisdom of God being spoken into our prayer time. It takes a willingness to hear and a heart that is in awe of God's presence.

> *"The Lord confides in those who fear him; he makes his covenant known to them. My eyes are ever on the Lord, for only he will release my feet from the snare." Psalm 25:14-15*

You will understand spiritual wisdom only if you accept the gift of the Holy Spirit. In 1 Corinthians 2:7-16, Paul explained this to the church of Corinth. He was giving them encouragement to ask God for revelation by quoting from the prophet Isaiah. 1 Corinthians 2:9-10 tells us, "However, as it is written: 'What no eye has seen, what no ear has heard, and what no human mind has conceived'—the things God has prepared for those who love him—these are the things God has revealed to us by his Spirit."

Renew Your Mind.

How will you know when God is answering your prayer? The best way to understand what someone is saying is to learn their language. Although my Bible is printed in English words, I still have to learn God's language. I recognize the words God uses in my Bible, but I must learn to understand His intent. I can understand God's answer to my prayer after I spend time renewing my mind.

> *"Do not conform to the pattern of this world, but be transformed by the renewing of your mind. Then you will be able to test and approve what God's will is—his good, pleasing and perfect will." Romans 12:2*

If your mind is having trouble understanding God's answer to your prayer, you can fix that by meditating on the Scriptures and listening to the Spirit of God. As you read the Scriptures, consider how the verses apply to what you've been praying about.

God wants us to know his will.

> *"Therefore do not be foolish, but understand what the Lord's will is."* Ephesians 5:17

If we renew our minds by reading God's word and listening to His Spirit, we will be able to recognize when God is giving us instruction. It takes time spent in His presence.

Joshua spent a lot of time with God when Moses was leading the people out of Egypt and into the Promised Land.

> *"The Lord would speak to Moses face to face, as one speaks to a friend. Then Moses would return to the camp, but his young aide Joshua son of Nun did not leave the tent."* Exodus 33:11

It makes sense that Joshua stayed in the tent. He was preparing to be a significant leader. God was preparing Joshua to continually seek Him for direction. Joshua's time in the presence of God was crucial for the success of God's plan.

How long are you willing to seek God? How long will you stay in God's presence?

There is no exact timetable. I can't tell you if you'll begin to hear from God in fifteen seconds, fifteen minutes, or fifteen days. Your determination to learn in God's presence is up to you and no one else.

The easy way to begin hearing God's answers to your prayers is to spend time seeking Him every day. Start your day with a twenty-minute prayer time. If that's not enough for you, expand that time according to your pleasure.

Speak prayers to God and write prayers to God. But don't sit and wait for God to initiate the conversation. Don't get bored or frustrated because God didn't talk to you.

If you went to visit your grandfather, would you just show up and sit there, waiting for him to do all the talking? No. You would tell him about what's been happening in your life.

Your kindness to your grandfather would make it easier to have a real conversation with him.

It's the same with God.

If you show up in your prayer time, showing God the fruit of the Spirit in your life and in your prayers, you'll see a positive response. You'll feel God's pleasure when you show how much you love Him.

Chapter 6 Action List

1. Write all the ways God has been responding to you.

2. Keep renewing your mind by studying Scripture and listening to the Spirit of God.

3. If you haven't already, start your daily prayer journaling habit.

CHAPTER SEVEN

Become accountable.

When God responds to your prayers, write down whatever God says or does. If He gives you instruction, write your plan of obedience.

Tip #10: Write your plan of obedience.

Your daily prayer journal will be filled with your words to God and how you see God acting and speaking in your life.

When you start hearing from God, it's understandable that you're not going to be perfect in your obedience. God is patient with all of His children.

The act of writing down how you will obey God's instruction will help you create a plan of action. You can make a checklist of steps included in that action and mark each step as you complete it.

Whatever it takes, be sure you make yourself accountable when you hear from God.

What does answered prayer look like?

It's different each time. God puts people together in places where it seems like an accident or a coincidence, but it's one of the ways God answers prayers.

For some people, God will cause you to hear His wisdom in your spirit during your prayer time.

For others, you might never hear God's voice when you pray. But that doesn't mean He's not responding to your prayers.

I know my mother-in-law was praying for God to give her grandchildren. I don't know this because she told me what she was praying for. She didn't. But God spoke to me and told me I would be pregnant. It didn't occur to me at the time, but doesn't that sound like an answer to the prayers of a woman who wanted grandchildren?

Your prayers change as your relationship with God develops over time. When God directs you to do something, your ability to act quickly improves as you mature.

Tip #11: Note the dates of answered prayer.

Make sure you write the date of when your prayers were answered. Write how God moved things together for you.

Maybe meeting a new friend isn't an answer to your prayer, but it might be an answer to your new friend's prayer.

When you see God's hand in your circumstances, think about how you can be a blessing to others. Remember that your job as God's child is to represent Him with love.

Chapter 7 Action List

1. List what God has instructed you to do.
2. Write your plan of obedience.
3. Write the date when your prayers were answered.
4. List the ways God has enabled you to be a blessing to others.

CHAPTER EIGHT

Wait for the answer.

By this time, we've prayed and we're confident that God is moving on our behalf to bring an answer to our prayers. So what do we do while we wait for the completion of the answer?

We already know how to revise the list of things we're praying about. Now it's time to find a verse that confirms our goal.

We don't always know if we're waiting on our own spiritual maturity or waiting on someone else to be in the right place at the right time. When we're waiting, we need encouragement.

God can direct us to a Bible verse that is related to our prayers. He's good at encouraging us when we're in that waiting period.

Tip #12: Write the verse.

Ask God for direction and write the Bible verse that God points out to you.

You can write it in your journal. But also write it on a note card to have it handy so you can memorize it while you wait for the completion of the answer.

God's encouragement will keep you focused on Him while the answer to prayer is being prepared in the background.

Have you ordered food at a restaurant and waited a long time for the food to be served? The kitchen employees were working on preparing your food the whole time. They didn't forget about you. Some things take longer to prepare than others.

"Be still, and know that I am God; I will be exalted among the nations, I will be exalted in the earth." Psalm 46:10

To me, this verse means: Calm down. Don't get in a rush. Focus on doing what I told you.

If the answer to your prayer takes a while, just remember that God will never forget you. He's still there.

And He knows what He's doing.

Chapter 8 Action List

1. Find a Bible verse that applies to your prayers.
2. Write the verse in your journal.
3. Write the verse on a note card so you can memorize it.

CONCLUSION

Write about your love for God.

Once you have journaled through these twelve tips over the course of a month, you can go back to the beginning of your journal and read through your answers to prayer. You can see how God has been leading you through the mountains and valleys in your life.

Then you can start again to see how your relationship with God improves over the next month.

Now that you know how the tips in this step-by-step process work together, take a day to write love poems to God—not asking for anything but simply being with God. That's a powerful way to show love to God.

SUMMARY

These are the twelve tips that will help you improve your relationship with God and see His answers to your prayers.

Ask God to help you through these tips.

1. List your needs.
2. Ask God to help you make corrections to the list.
3. Look for examples of how God has answered prayers in the past.
4. Raise your expectation of what God may do.
5. Look at how God sees you.
6. Look at how you see God.
7. Ask God how you need to change.
8. Ask God to help you prioritize what you're praying for.
9. Listen for what God is saying to you in response.
10. Write your plan of obedience and hold yourself accountable.
11. Write the dates when your prayers were answered and what that answered prayer looked like.
12. Write and memorize Scripture while you wait.

CONGRATULATIONS!

You've finished the book!

Now that you've read this book and enjoyed your own personal success, take a couple of minutes to write a review.

One way to tell others that the book has practical, easy-to-follow tips for people who want to improve their prayer lives is to post your review. Your honest opinion will be appreciated by people who are looking for help in this area.

Another way is to buy a copy of this book for a friend and tell them yourself how the book affected you.

FOR YOU!

Subscribers are the first to know about new releases, book sales, and giveaways. Sign up now for my Nonfiction Readers Club at *BookHip.com/KLXVDX*.

My gift to you is a free digital prayer journal. It's available exclusively for subscribers.

You'll also get educational and promotional emails to help you build a legacy of kindness.

BOOKS BY LAURA DOMINO

NONFICTION

Heroine: Rising to the Challenge: Strengthen your heroic traits. After 25 days of accepting the fun goals, you'll be the heroine you've always wanted to be.

5 Powerful Ways to Show Love: Strengthen your relationships by showing love to God and people. Loving your neighbor just got easier.

Prayers That Work: Strengthen your prayer life! Learn the twelve tips that will transform your prayers. Energize your prayer life with this step-by-step process that helps your prayers go from self-focused to God-focused.

The Prayers That Work Journal: This is the companion journal to *Prayers That Work*.

The 4 Steps to Living Like a Superhero Series: This series addresses ways to show up with kindness for your family, friends, coworkers, and neighbors through all of life's seasons.

Scriptures and Scribbles (blue): This lined journal has places to list people you're praying for. Take it to church and use it as a sermon notes journal.

Scriptures and Scribbles (green): This unlined journal is easy to take to church or a Bible study. Draw charts or write notes to encourage yourself.

FICTION

The Fulton Ridge Christian Romance Series: This contemporary Christian romance series of standalone novels has conflict and love but no sex or foul language. Get to know the characters in this fictional Texas town and see how they find true love.

One Man's Haven: The Protector Series Book One: Enjoy the first book in the series, and then read the rest of the series. This contemporary Christian romantic suspense novel has love and intrigue but no sex or foul language. Sharla's life has taken a downward spiral. How will she decide between a bodyguard and a billionaire when she needs a safe haven?

ABOUT THE AUTHOR

Laura Domino writes books that help you build your character, your relationships, and you prayer life.

She encourages people to use their own uniqueness while building kindness in their communities. Having volunteered locally and internationally, she's experienced the thrill of helping people. Now she shares the joy of serving through her books.

Contact her at LauraDomino.com

Made in the USA
Monee, IL
11 June 2024

59616191R00030